EFFECTIVE
SURVIVAL STRATEGIES™

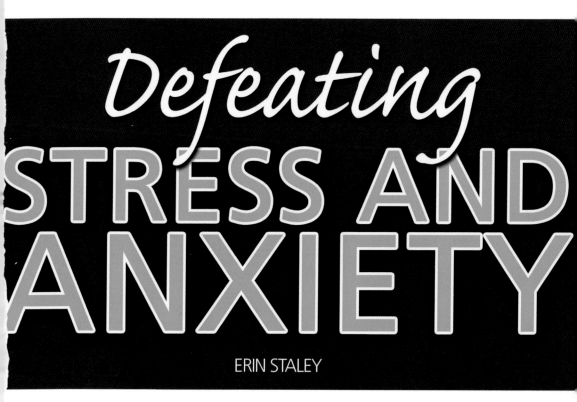

Defeating
STRESS AND
ANXIETY

ERIN STALEY

ROSEN
PUBLISHING®
New York

Published in 2016 by The Rosen Publishing Group, Inc.
29 East 21st Street, New York, NY 10010

Library of Congress Cataloging-in-Publication Data

Staley, Erin.
 Defeating stress and anxiety / Erin Staley. — First edition.
     pages cm. — (Effective survival strategies)
 Audience: Grades 7–12.
 Includes bibliographical references and index.
 ISBN 978-1-4994-6195-4 (library bound)
 1. Stress management—Juvenile literature. I. Title.
 RA785.S74 2016
 155.9'042—dc23
                             2015024818

For many of the images in this book, the people photographed are models. The depictions do not imply actual situations or events.

Manufactured in China

Contents

Introduction

Finding a date for the prom. Getting good grades. Raising enough money to pay for a car. Caring for a loved one. Filling your schedule with as many extracurricular activities as possible in order to get into the right college, get the right job, and live the perfect life. Yes, these are all highly stressful considerations for young people, just like you. But it doesn't end there. You have internal pressures, too. A growing body. Peer pressures. Coming to terms with your sexual identity. The need to fit in and how to handle it if you don't. It's no wonder teens today are experiencing high levels of stress and anxiety.

When tension is high, you may want to scream, act up, or pull away from friends and family. You may be tempted to give up, give in, or turn to destructive solutions, such as violence, drugs, or alcohol. But you can overcome stress and anxiety with a little courage and a lot of information-based action.

In this resource, you'll discover what stress really is, how stressors can fuel the tension, and how stress can affect your body. You'll read about celebrities who have dealt with or who are dealing with stress and anxiety in their own special ways. You will discover the difference between good stress and harmful stress and figure out what you can do when symptoms flare up. You will learn about anxiety, its disorders, and what can be done

Your thoughts can either calm you down or stress you out. Take time each day to consider which thoughts are serving you and which should be cast aside.

to manage thoughts, feelings, and behaviors for optimum wellness. You will also receive a list of local and national resources for coping solutions and help from others who will listen, understand, and offer the help you're seeking. Finally, you will gain the know-how to help others find workable solutions—both online and off-line—for a lifetime of stress- and anxiety-free living.

Rest assured, everyone has "been there, done that" when it comes to stress and anxiety. But the key to getting beyond it is to identify the stressors in your life and what steps will keep them at bay. The more you know, the better you'll be able to care for yourself now and in the future. And what's more, you'll be able to get on with the fulfilling life you want and deserve.

CHAPTER 1

STRESS 101

A little stress can keep you motivated, helping you to reach your goals. However, if you feel overwhelmed, give yourself a time out to rest and rejuvenate.

Overwhelmed? In a rush? No time to sleep, study, or hang out with friends? You're not alone. All across the country, teens just like you are juggling the challenges of life. Advanced placement (AP) classes, after-school activities, volunteer obligations, religious outings, and family gatherings—it's a lot to keep track of. You have to make the grade, make the team, make enough money for college, and make everyone happy. No wonder the number of stressed-out teens is on the rise.

HOW TO STOP THE BULLIES

Stress affects teens in a big way, and USAToday.com's Sharon Jayson notes just how much. She cites an online survey of 1,018 U.S.-based teenagers (ages thirteen to seventeen) and 1,950 adults (ages eighteen and older). When the findings were compared between age groups, stress levels of teens mirrored stress levels of adults. In addition, teens admitted to the following responses when faced with stressful situations:

- 59 percent reported that balancing activities was a "somewhat or very significant stressor."
- 40 percent experienced anger or irritability.
- 40 percent ignored home responsibilities.
- 36 percent felt nervous or anxious.
- 32 percent experienced headaches.
- 26 percent noticed a change in sleep habits.
- 26 percent were short when they spoke with peers.
- 21 percent neglected school or work because of stress levels.

Jayson goes on to note: "A third [of teens] say stress makes them feel overwhelmed, depressed or sad. Teen girls are more stressed than boys, just as women nationally are more stressed than men." The report indicates that stress affects adolescents into adulthood. If these statistics closely resemble your experiences, keep reading. There are many coping solutions you can use to let go of stress and lead a more balanced life.

What Is Stress?

The American Academy of Pediatrics (AAP) defines stress as "the uncomfortable feeling you get when you're worried, scared, angry, frustrated, or overwhelmed." Stress is the body's reaction to a trigger and its attempt to restore balance between the mind and body. When the trigger is gone, stress disappears. When stress is excessive—lasting longer than six months—it can turn into anxiety, a condition discussed in chapter two.

Triggering Stress

Stress is brought on by triggers, also known as stressors. They're either internal or external. Internal triggers are thoughts and feelings, such as a poor self-image, moral misjudgment, sexual tendencies, and perfectionism. External triggers are pressures, circumstances, and expectations from others. They can include a breakup, a news report, chronic illness, the death of a loved one, separation or divorce, financial hardship, or a troubled home life.

PUTTING LIFE INTO PERSPECTIVE

Diapered, bibbed, and suffering from bottle rot, five-year-old Tammie was neglected by her biological parents. They were addicts and often left her in a playpen in their cockroach-infested apartment. Malnourished and delayed from a lack of stimulus, Tammie was placed in foster care. In six years, Tammie lived in six different foster homes with two near-adoptions.

LaRae *(left)* and her daughter, Tammie *(right)*, work as a team to manage stress and anxiety. They use coping solutions for optimum health and well-being at home, work, school, and play.

She developed a fear of interrogation or being questioned, a desperation for friends, and a plan to stash money.

One morning, Tammie's then foster parent demanded that the eleven-year-old pack her belongings. A new foster mother, LaRae, was introduced to her, and a move was scheduled for the following day. Tammie was confused; but when she stepped up to LaRae's door, a tail-wagging Matilda greeted her. A purring Sophie soon followed, and Tammie knew she'd like living with her new foster mother. Anyone who loved animals as much as she did must be special.

In her new home, Tammie continued to face stressful situations. She had academic obligations, as well as chaperoned visits with her biological mother and endless meetings with social workers. In response, she sleepwalked, craved

(contiued on the next page)

(continued from previous page)

hugs, and required a constant night-light. When LaRae brought up adoption, Tammie's loyalty to her biological mother became apparent. But when the woman exclaimed, "Thank goodness, my daughter's finally going to be adopted," the papers were soon filed.

Tammie believes her past has helped her face everyday stressors, such as tests, relationships, and post–high school plans. "I *would've b*een dead," she says, "but I've forgiven. I'm not grateful for my past, but it's helped put things into perspective."

Today, the teenager relieves stress by cuddling with Matilda and Sophie, performing in musicals, listening to playlists, satisfying a sweet tooth, and hanging out with a tight circle of friends. "I feel like I can overcome anything," says Tammie. "I'm really grateful for my home life and faith; and I tell myself that everything's going to be okay. Then I have some chocolate. It's a good life!"

Stress Symptoms

When stress strikes, the body can't help but react. It has an innate need to return to a state of calm. It will alert you when relief is needed, and these alerts can be physical or mental symptoms. Physical symptoms include a change in appetite, restlessness, achy muscles, clammy hands, shortness of breath, or lightheadedness. Mental symptoms might include nervousness, distraction, worry, irritability, anger, or a feeling of being overwhelmed. All of these symptoms are normal and can affect us often during our lives.

Beyond the Glitz and Glamour

While it may seem that your favorite celebrities are living a posh life with movie conflicts, music deals, clothing lines, and exotic trips, they face enormous amounts of internal and external stress. Like us, celebrities look for tension-busting solutions. Singer, songwriter, and Grammy Award winner Taylor Swift turns to songwriting. She tells Lizzy Goodman of *Elle*, "It's me sitting on my bed feeling pain I didn't understand, writing a song, and understanding it better." Swift goes on to say, "It's just something I do to feel better." Another singer, songwriter, and Grammy Award winner, John Mayer, always keeps antianxiety prescription medication in his pocket. Comedian, producer, actress, and author Tina Fey turns to humor. In her autobiography, *Bossypants*, she tells readers: "'Blorft' is an adjective I just made up that means 'Completely overwhelmed but proceeding as if everything is fine and reacting to the stress with the torpor of a possum.' I have been blorft every day for the past seven years."

Other celebrities take a break. Academy Award winner, filmmaker, and humanitarian Angelina Jolie turns to meditation. The actress tells *Stylist* magazine, "I find meditation in sitting on the floor with the kids coloring for an hour, or going on the trampoline. You do something you love, that makes you happy, and that gives you your meditation." Zayn Malik of the English-Irish boy band One Direction quit the band's world tour when rumors flew that he cheated on his fiancée, Perrie Edwards. He flew home to the United Kingdom to recover. *Jersey Shore* reality television star Vinny Guadagnino took time off from filming the show's fifth season. He'd been dealing with panic attacks since high school and recognized the reemergence of symptoms. Guadagnino explains his decision to take a break in an MTV Act video: "It's

Jennifer Lawrence, the actor known for her roles in *The Hunger Games* and *Silver Linings Playbook*, speaks freely about her anxiety as a child.

a terrible environment for me to be in when I'm anxious because there's drinking involved, there's fighting involved, a lack of sleep, a lack of privacy." Guadagnino goes on to say, "When my anxiety starts to interfere with my job, my school, or things that I do in my every day life, it starts to become a problem." Guadagnino took the time to rebalance and then teamed up with the Jed Foundation to help others with similar conditions.

Like Guadagnino, Oscar-winning actress Jennifer Lawrence suffered from anxiety as a youth.

USMagazine.com's Allison Takeda shares Lawrence's story:

> I was hyperactive, curious about everything. When my mother told me about my childhood, she always told me there was like a light in me, a spark that inspired me constantly. When I entered school, the light went out. We never knew what it was, a kind of social anxiety. But I had friends.

Lawrence goes on to say:

> One day, I begged my parents to take me to a casting [call]. We went to New York, and that's where I started acting. Just on stage, my mother saw the change that was taking place in me. She saw my anxieties disappear. She found her daughter, the one who had this light and joy

before school. I finally found a way [to] open the door to a universe that I understood, that was good for me and made me happy, because I felt capable, whereas before I felt worthless.

McKayla Maroney, the 2012 Olympic gold medal winner in artistic gymnastics, deals with constant pressures to be the best in her sport. She shared her favorite coping solutions with *Huffington Post*'s Carolyn Gregoire:

McKayla Maroney inspired fans with this 2015 tweet: "don't [sic] let the drama, stress, and craziness of this world distract you from the beauty, bliss, and love that exists everywhere."

> Sometimes, I just have to be alone for a little bit...I think my favorite thing to do is just watch something funny on TV and take a shower. I like to take my laptop and go on Twitter and Instagram, but sometimes you have to stay off of it too because not everything is positive. And I cannot read the comments. No, no, no. That's a very bad idea.

Maroney continues:

> There's a lot of stress out there, and to handle it, you just need to believe in yourself, always go back to the person that you know you are and don't let anybody tell you any different, because everyone's special and everyone's awesome.

CHAPTER 2

WHAT'S HAPPENING ON THE INSIDE

The body is a magnificent, fine-tuned structure. It contains many systems, such as the digestive, muscular, and reproductive, to maximize body function. When stress and anxiety strike, the endocrine and nervous systems jump into action to alert you to take action.

The Stress Response

When internal and external triggers get you riled up, the brain's hypothalamus starts a chain reaction called the stress response. It tells the adrenal glands to make two hormones: cortisol and adrenaline. Cortisol, also known as the stress hormone, calculates the presence and strength of stress. Adrenaline allows you to respond to the stress. Both cortisol and adrenaline are released into the bloodstream, causing your breathing to quicken, your heart to race, and your metabolism to speed up. Blood vessels widen, allowing blood to pump to large muscle groups. This gets the body ready to drop, run, dive, or attack. Pupils dilate to improve vision, and the liver releases glucose to increase the body's energy.

The Good, the Bad, and the Exhilarating

Stress is like spice—in the right proportion it enhances the flavor of a dish.

Too little produces a bland, dull meal; too much may choke you. —Donald Tubesing

Although this book focuses on ways to defeat stress and anxiety, it's also important to note that stress isn't always a bad thing. It can keep you excited, ready for adventure. Think about the thrill you get when watching a scary movie, attending a school dance, or hanging upside down on a roller coaster. The stress you experience during these moments is referred to as eustress. Hans Selye (1907–1982), an endocrinologist and human stress researcher, coined the phrase. He blended the word "stress" with the Greek word, *eu*, meaning "well" or "good." Besides the thrill of entertainment, eustress can also motivate you to overcome challenges and achieve goals. Consider the stress you feel before taking the stage to play a lead role, making the game-winning shot, or getting behind the wheel to take a driving exam. Without stress in small doses, life would be boring and without purpose.

THE FIGHT-OR-FLIGHT RESPONSE

There you are, hanging out with friends on a camping trip, when rustling leaves catch your attention. Is danger lurking nearby? You'll have to decide quickly whether to stay and fight or to escape. But don't worry, physical reactions in your body will make it possible to do either. This is called the fight-or-flight response, and it has allowed humans to survive since the beginning of time. When hungry predators approached, early humans experienced on-the-spot physical changes. Adrenal glands pumped adrenaline.

The fight-or-flight response is an internal warning system. It alerts you to external threats that are—or could be—harmful or even dangerous.

Breathing quickened. Muscles tensed up. And blood raced to the arms and legs. Even the senses, such as vision, smell, and hearing, sharpened.

Today, humans experience these same fight-or-flight responses. You'll recognize them when confronted by a bully, receiving criticism, running late for an important date, or saving someone's life. Fight-or-flight reactions are quite normal; but should they continue for a long period of time, they can negatively affect your cardiovascular and digestive systems. They can even disturb your sleep.

There are treatments—prescribed by a medical professional—that will help to restore the body to its pre-fight-or-flight state. Breathing exercises are one such treatment. The idea is to calm the mind and body through purposeful breathing. Find a quiet location, and either sit in a straight-backed chair or lie on the floor. Take a deep breath and fill the lungs with as much oxygen as possible. Then exhale slowly to release physical tension. Repeat the inhalation/exhalation process for one minute. As you feel more comfortable with the exercise, you can build up to five minutes of relaxation and rebalancing.

Long-Term Stress

If a threat—real or perceived—persists, your nervous system will stay in active mode. Hormones will continue to course through your system, and your body will become confused. It won't be able to reset itself. Eventually, this will wear the body down and cause a ripple effect of symptoms. Mentally, you'll feel overwhelmed, irritable, and moody. Cortisol will lower your body's

You may not always "feel" excessive stress, but you could experience long-term symptoms. These can include headaches, hair loss, acne, eating disorders, gastrointestinal problems, cardiovascular disease, and sexual dysfunction.

serotonin (the mood-balancing chemical) and dopamine (the reward-motivated chemical that inspires action). This could lead to depression. Physically, you'll experience headaches, difficulty sleeping, high blood pressure, stomach issues, chest pain, a weakened immune system, and allergic reactions. You'll be wound up or worried on a regular basis, overreacting to difficulties—both big and small. Everything will feel like a crisis. If this reaction lasts longer than six months, it could turn into an anxiety disorder.

UNDERSTANDING PANIC ATTACKS

There you are, at the mall with friends, when your heart begins to pound. You start trembling and hyperventilating, and it feels as if you're about to die. You rush to the doctor only to learn you've had a panic attack. MayoClinic.org describes this condition as "a sudden epi- sode of intense fear that triggers severe physical reactions when there is no real danger or apparent cause." This medi- cal condition is normal and can happen at least once or twice in a person's lifetime.

Panic attacks come on without warning and last for approximately ten minutes. Symptoms typically show up in the late teens or early adulthood, and they are difficult to manage without medical treatment. The cause has yet to be pinpointed, but researchers believe intense stress, genetics, and changes in brain function can play a major role. If you feel like you may have experienced a panic attack or have symptoms, talk with a medical professional immediately. You will want to start a treatment plan consisting of psycho- therapy and medication. It is important to note that if you find yourself fearing panic attacks, you may be at risk for a condition known as panic disorder.

Anxiety and Its Disorders

As stress is the body's short-term reaction to triggers, anxiety is the body's long-term reaction to stress. Anxiety is a mental disorder, which can include generalized anxiety disorder (GAD), panic disorder, post-traumatic stress disorder (PTSD), obses- sive-compulsive disorder (OCD), and social anxiety. These are complex disorders and are thought to be caused by genetics,

Mild anxiety is normal. However, intense anxiety is an overwhelming feeling of fear, worry, and dread of what may happen. If allowed to linger, it can lead to anxiety disorders.

psychological factors, developmental issues, and environmental conditions. Some of the studies sponsored by the National Institute of Mental Health (NIMH) have shown that unlike other anxiety disorders, PTSD is brought on by trauma.

According to the NIMH, "Anxiety disorders affect about 40 million American adults age 18 years and older (about 18%) in a given year, causing them to be filled with fearfulness and uncertainty." They go on to report the findings of a national survey of adolescent mental health: "About 8 percent of teens ages 13–18 have an anxiety disorder, with symptoms commonly emerging around age 6. However, of these teens, only 18 percent received mental health care."

Symptoms of anxiety disorders depend on the person but typically include irrational fear, dread, depression, and substance abuse. But with early detection, the symptoms can be treated. If you think you have an anxiety disorder, consult a medical professional. He or she will perform a full diagnostic evaluation. If a disorder is diagnosed, a plan of treatment will be recommended. It could include one or more of the following: cognitive-behavioral therapy (CBT), prescription medications, and coping solutions.

Treating Anxiety Disorders

CBT is the most common therapy used to treat anxiety disorders. According to HelpGuide.org, CBT "addresses negative patterns and distortions in the way we look at the world and ourselves." It is a combination of cognitive therapy (exploring how your thoughts contribute to anxiety) and behavior therapy (determining how your actions trigger anxiety). CBT is administered by a psychologist, psychiatrist, counselor, or social worker. Over the course of several months, patients are guided through high-anxiety situations. For example, an OCD patient would be encouraged to get his hands dirty, wait, and then wash them when directed. The idea is to gradually extend the waiting period until the OCD disorder disappears. A PTSD patient would be asked to recall the trauma that triggered the disorder. This recollection would be performed in a safe, supportive environment, with hopes that the disorder would be resolved.

Medications are prescribed to lessen the physical symptoms of anxiety disorders. Common medications include antianxiety drugs, antidepressants, and beta-blockers. Although medication doesn't cure anxiety disorders, it can help patients lead a normal, fulfilling life. Coping solutions are also recommended by medical professionals and will be addressed in the following chapters.

CHAPTER 3

QUICK AND EASY COPING SOLUTIONS

According to USAToday.com's Sharon Jayson, "More than a quarter (27%) [of teenagers] say they experience 'extreme stress' during the school year, vs. 13% in the summer. And 34% expect stress to increase in the coming year." Unfortunately, teens don't always know how to manage their stress. That is, until now. This chapter offers ways to cope with stress and anxiety in a safe and healthy manner.

Find the Right Coping Solution

Coping solutions—the methods you use to sidestep turmoil and relax—reverse the effects of "fight, flight, or freeze." They slow down your heart rate, blood flow, and breathing. Some of the following solutions detailed in this chapter will make sense for you, and some won't. That's OK. Not every coping solution does the job for every person. Just be open, and once you find the right solution for you, watch how quickly stress levels decrease. You'll feel better, and you will become more satisfied with who you are and the decisions you are making.

It's All in Your Head

Have you ever had a challenge haunt you? It sticks in your brain so long that all you can think about is how you handled it and what you would do differently? Did this challenge seem to grow out of control the more you considered it? If so, don't worry. This internal chitter chatter—also known as self talk—is normal. It can be positive, building you up, or negative, weighing you down. The good news is that there's a way to turn negative self talk into positive talk by changing your thoughts.

Actor, director, and producer Goldie Hawn had this to say on *Katie Couric*: "Stress is something that is created in the mind, basically; and it's how we look at things. So our greatest defense against stress is actually the ability to change our mind or change our thinking." To manage your stress, Hawn encourages us to change the way we think. You can do this by putting only positive thoughts in your mind. For inspiration, reach out to positive-minded friends, family, teachers, and counselors or therapists. You can even go online to find inspiring quotations, helpful affirmations, calming prayers, uplifting song lyrics, and handy apps. And if that isn't enough, just take a deep breath and say, "Everything's going to be OK."

Develop Strong Communication Skills

Being able to express yourself—to share what you think and feel—can relieve a great deal of tension. State your thoughts and feelings in a firm but polite manner when facing stressful

Avoid stressful assumptions and misunderstandings by using effective communication skills. Commit to sharing from the heart and listening without judgment.

situations. A simple "I feel lonely when you don't reach out," or "I am disappointed when you continue to stand me up" could do the trick. If you feel a little awkward about starting, find a private space in which to practice. Before you know it, you'll be able to express yourself with confidence.

S-l-o-w D-o-w-n

One of the best ways to cope with stress and anxiety is to slow down. Viggo Mortensen, actor, musician, artist, and poet, weighed in on this coping solution by sharing the following with Chitra Ramaswamy of the *Scotsman*:

> One of the best pieces of advice I ever got was from a horse master. He told me to go slow to go fast. I think that

Looking for ways to slow down? Take a hot bath. Go for a run. Pick up a hobby. Or spend some time with a cherished pet.

applies to everything in life. We live as though there aren't enough hours in the day but if we do each thing calmly and carefully we will get it done quicker and with much less stress.

Once you slow down, you can address any situation objectively. You might even discover ways to compartmentalize the issue into smaller, easy-to-tackle tasks. If you can't slow down, at least take a break. Five minutes. An hour. A week. Whatever it takes to catch your breath and refresh. Of course, this isn't license to procrastinate or to abandon your responsibilities. It's just a breather before you're ready to get back into the situation.

Treat Yourself to Daily Meditation

Meditation quiets the mind and calms the body. It turns down the noise of outside sources—e-mails, phone calls, the noisy neighbor across the street—and offers complete rest from head to toe. There are many ways to meditate, but the most simple way to start is to make a plan. Start by deciding which time of day works best. Then choose a quiet location in which to sit or kneel. You may want a cushion or chair for added comfort. Some people light a candle or play soothing instrumental music to create a calming atmosphere. Next, close your eyes and purposely relax your muscles. Bring your focus inward, as you inhale through the nose and exhale through the mouth. Notice your breathing and the way your body responds to the exercise. If your mind wanders, bring it back. Try this for five minutes at first. As you get used to meditating, you will be able to handle additional time. Once you get the hang of it, you'll find that your day isn't complete without a meditation session to rejuvenate your mind and body.

Project Relaxation

Maxed out? Quiet your mind and body with relaxing activities. Meditate. Read for pleasure. Take advantage of the ancient healing art of massage. Paint, draw, or write a novel. Find those things that will bring joy to your day and that are easy to build into a busy schedule. You can also try breathing exercises. For example, take a slow, deep inhalation through your nose. Hold it for a few seconds and then slowly exhale through your mouth. Repeat. Your body will begin to relax, and your mind will slow down. If you like the results, try additional breathing exercises you find online.

Get Up and Go

We all know that regular exercise can do a world of good for your cardiovascular system, immune system, and weight management. But it's also a stress buster. Exercise can help overcome edginess and tension while calming blood pressure, loosening muscles, and pushing toxins out of the body. What's more, it can offer a welcome distraction. First Lady Michelle Obama, wife of the president of the United States, has employed exercise as her coping solution. She tells Marie Claire: "Exercise is really important to me—it's therapeutic. So if I'm ever feeling tense or stressed or like I'm about to have a meltdown, I'll put on my iPod and head to the gym or out on a bike ride along Lake Michigan with the girls."

Unfortunately, teens are not getting enough exercise according to a study described in Sharon Jayson's USAToday.com article: "Only about 37% of teens surveyed exercise or walk to manage stress; 28% play sports. Many more choose what experts say

Physical activity is not only fun and healthy, but it lowers stress and anxiety. For added enjoyment, invite your friends to join in the workout!

are less healthy activities, including playing video games (46%) and spending time online (43%)." These digital activities in and of themselves are not harmful; in fact, this resource goes into great detail about the benefits of online options for stress relief. While we'll explore these options in the next chapter, it's important to bear in mind that too much of any one thing is excessive. As human beings, we function best when balance is achieved.

Fuel Up

Nourish your body with nutrient-rich foods every day, and you'll be energized to take on the stressors of life. According to ChooseMyPlate.gov, we need to fill our plates with five food

SHORT-TERM FIXES

When faced with mounting stress, some adults and teens turn to alcohol as well as prescription and illegal drugs. While these substances can make you feel different or maybe even forget your troubles, these effects are temporary. The buzz or high eventually wears off, and not only do you have to deal with the same situation, but you have to cope with withdrawal or a hangover. Short-term fixes such as these actually stress out the body by wearing down its internal systems. This can throw a major kink into your mind's ability to bounce back. Instead, try a healthier approach: go surfing, shop online, or pick up a game of basketball. Try any one of the coping solutions described in this book to feel better and move forward.

groups: fruits, vegetables, grains, proteins, and dairy products. Age, gender, and amount of physical activity will determine your recommended daily intake. And of course, a regular diet of home-cooked meals always helps fight stress and anxiety. Skip foods high in fat, salt, and sugar—which often means avoiding those convenient fast food meals. Quick bites tend to be low in the vitamins and minerals a stressed body needs. Then partner your meals with eight glasses of water a day to avoid dehydration, as this condition tends to aggravate the body.

Laugh It Up

Finally, chisel out some free time to be with your favorite people. Do the things you love to do on a regular basis. Rock out on the drums. Bake a scrumptious chocolate cake. Play the back nine.

Laughter is the best medicine when it comes to overcoming stress and anxiety. It releases feel-good endorphins and brings you closer to friends and family.

Surprise your bestie with a manicure/pedicure. Whatever it is, be sure to mix in some sidesplitting laughter. Laughter is a fantastic stress buster. It has short- and long-term benefits for both mind and body. It intensifies oxygen intake, gets your heart and lungs pumping, and elevates endorphins to ease pain and discomfort. Laughter also stimulates circulation and relaxes your muscles, both of which minimize the physical symptoms of stress. Your mood will improve, and you'll feel so much happier.

Get Your Give On

Another stress buster is helping others. Not only does it serve as a distraction from your own troubles, but it builds confidence, gives your life greater purpose, and helps you to connect with others. Give of your time, talents, and resources. This could involve mowing a neighbor's lawn, tutoring children with learning disabilities, or volunteering at a local food bank. Giving is also a great way to relieve the stress of others.

Count Your ZZZs

Teenagers grow and develop at lightning speed. Their bodies require a healthy—and consistent—amount of sleep. Nine hours a night is recommended, while eight hours a night is sufficient. Unfortunately, teenagers average only 7.4 hours of sleep on any given school night, according to the American Psychological Association's Stress in America Survey. That's not enough to keep your skin aglow, to stay emotionally balanced, to concentrate at a higher level, or to face your stressors. Plus, a shift in your circadian rhythm—a twenty-four-hour cycle of human biological activity—causes you to want to stay up and sleep in late. But you can maximize your chances of getting a sound sleep every night by skipping caffeinated beverages later in the day and cutting back on screen time right before bed. Before falling asleep, read, listen to relaxing music, or meditate. Just be sure to maintain a regular sleep schedule by going to sleep and waking up at the same time every day.

CHAPTER 4

UNPLUG BY PLUGGING IN

When you're ready to blow off some steam, try plugging in to a mobile device, personal computer (PC), or video game station. You'll enjoy some escapism, while getting your mind off stress and anxiety.

In the Zone

Epic beats, jaw-dropping explosions, hypnotic graphics, and gripping storylines make video games a huge draw for those in pursuit of eustress. Games make everything seem trivial, which could be exactly what you need when tension is high. If you're a gamer, you probably have your favorites. But if you need suggestions, try these favorites. *Myst III: Exile* allows you to explore mysterious environments and solve puzzles. *Sid Meier's Civilization V* lets you rule the world by creating new civilizations. Get behind the wheel with *Euro Truck Simulator 2* and take on Europe's adventurous motorways. *Sherlock Holmes: Crimes and*

Gaming with a friend or within a virtual social community can help you blow off some steam. It can also help you gain confidence, develop trust, and build teamwork skills.

Punishments is perfect for those who want to immerse themselves in the faraway adventure of a British crime drama. *Take On Mars* is a simulator that lets you explore the surface of a red planet aboard rovers and landers. If you're a golf lover, knock around a few balls on the rolling greens of *The Golf Club. Flower* lets you travel on the wind, collecting petals. *Minecraft's* creative mode lets you build without the threat of attacking mobs. *Journey* soothes with a seamless story of an ancient civilization. Then there are the classics. *Donkey Kong, Pac-Man Championship Edition*, and *Super Mario World* offer fun, relaxation, and light-hearted competition.

Celebrities, such as Emma Watson, are not immune to stress. They use coping solutions to manage it, inspiring others to do the same.

App Your Way to Zen

Applications, also known as apps, allow you to de-stress at home or on the go. Visit your app store to find puzzles and word games. Try Words with Bookworm to build your vocabulary and satisfy your competitive spirit. Zone out with the mindless popping of Bubble Wrap. Create a calming retreat in Bejeweled's Relax in Zen mode or play cognitive mini-games to boost memory and attention skills with Lumosity. If you're ready to get lost in a zen moment, try Epic Zen Garden. Drag your finger across a koi pond and discover how quickly the fish will follow your lead. Rake patterns in the sand of the tranquil rock garden. Paint petals on the branches of a Sakura tree. Then watch as water from a garden well turns into a whirlwind of butterflies. Omvana offers more than five hundred downloadable audio tracks for guided meditation, hypnosis, and sleep. Headspace—an app used by actors Emma Watson and Gwyneth Paltrow—offers a free Take10 program. Simply plug in ten minutes a day for ten days to release mental expectations and physical tension.

THE SOUND-TRACK OF NATURE

Believe it or not, nature sounds can take relaxation to a whole new level. Just ask His Royal Highness the Duke of Cambridge KG KT, Prince William of England. In an interview with RadioTimes, Prince William revealed that animal sounds relax him:

I do regularly daydream, and Africa is definitely one of the places I go to. I've got hundreds of animals on my iPhone, noises and sounds of the bush, so if I am having a stressful day, I'll put a buffalo, a cricket or a newt on and it takes you back instantly to the bush. And it does completely settle me down.

Natural sound curator Cheryl Tipp of the British Library responds to Prince William's preferences by stating the following on TheGuardian.com:

We all have our favourites—whether that be a beautiful bird song, the churring of grasshoppers, a rhythmic frog chorus, lapping waves or the calls of buffalo. Sound is incredibly evocative and has the power to instantly transport us to another place. As Africa holds such a special place in William's heart, it's not surprising that the sounds of these species have the ability to relieve any stress that he's feeling, although I can't say that they would work for me!

You can find all sorts of nature sounds on websites, apps, and YouTube channels. Be sure to check out *RainBirdHD's* heavy rains and thunder—a full ten hours of ambient nature sounds to help with sleep, meditation, and relaxation. These can put you in a relaxed state as your cram for a test, frost cakes for the bake sale, write a book report, or recuperate from an injury.

Online stress-busters—in the form of relaxation websites, apps, and games—can bring peace and sanity to your daily routine. They make for the perfect "anytime, anywhere" getaway for the mind.

Get Connected for Relaxation

If picking up a yoga class or spending the afternoon in a day spa sounds calming, then check out MINDBODY Connect. It uses Google Maps functionality—along with a friendly design—to pinpoint classes, salons, spas, and gyms in your area. Book and pay with the click of a button. If you prefer an in-home experience, Zeel Massage On Demand delivers a licensed massage therapist to your doorstep in as little as an hour. Reserve and pay for a sixty- or ninety-minute massage, and before you know it, you'll be indulging in a Swedish or deep tissue massage in the comfort of your home.

Engage with Volunteerism

Stress can leave one feeling lost, without a purpose, and surviving from one day to the next. Volunteerism—the giving of one's time, resources, and talents to others—can change all of that. Volunteerism gives life meaning. It can also make stress more manageable, especially when you're having fun and bringing happiness to others.

Volunteerism opportunities are all around, at schools, community buildings, health care centers, and churches. You can clean an animal shelter, help an elderly neighbor with lawn care, or serve hot meals at a food bank. If you'd like additional ideas, plug in to online organizations. VolunteerMatch.org matches "good people" with "good causes." Kids, teens, and adults are welcome to search its data bank for volunteer opportunities that inspire them. Choose from more than thirty thousand opportunities around the world. You could become a dog socializer, host an exchange student, spread awareness about multiple sclerosis, prepare goodie bags for Bike to Work Day, or volunteer in Latin America this summer!

Another volunteerism option is with the United Nations (UN). This organization "contributes to peace and development through volunteerism worldwide" and offers in-person and online volunteerism experiences. If you're between the ages of eighteen and twenty-nine and are passionate about global peace and development, you can join the UN Youth Volunteer program. Help a local government, an international nonprofit organization, or an educational institution. If you blog, share your know-how as a volunteer blogger. If you design, use your creativity as a volunteer designer. If you're bilingual, translate helpful documents. You can even work assignments into your schedule, from anywhere in the world. The commitment itself lasts from six months to two years. All you need is volunteering experience in your school or community. If you're not eighteen years old just yet, you can prepare by volunteering right now. Gain valuable experience and then apply to the UN Youth Volunteer program when you're of age.

CHAPTER 5

SUPPORT AT YOUR FINGERTIPS

When stress strikes, it's tempting to feel that you're the only one in the world who is overwhelmed, challenged, and ready to pull your hair out. But you're not. There are many people that have gone through what you're going through. They want to help, and all you have to do is ask.

Reach Out to Your Network

When you're ready to reach out for support, consider those with whom you live, work, study, or play. This is called your network. It's a collection of trusted friends, family members, and neighbors who can share their "been there, done that" experiences. They can even pass along new coping strategies to weave into your stress management collection. If there's no one to confide in, or if you think you'll be judged, perhaps it's time to reach beyond your network. Counselors, therapists, medical doctors, and mental health professionals can talk through concerns, dissect the source of stress, and brainstorm possible solutions. These professionals are trained to listen objectively, make scientifically grounded recommendations, help you set boundaries, and offer realistic coping strategies.

Medications May Help

Sometimes medical professionals prescribe meditations to help with stress and anxiety symptoms. Antidepressants, such as Zoloft and Paxil, relieve depression and anxiety symptoms, improve concentration, and restore sleep. Antianxiety medications, also known as benzodiazepines, temporarily relieve severe

If you feel the long-term effects of stress and anxiety, talk to your doctor about prescription medications and natural remedies. These may prove helpful in minimizing symptoms and avoiding anxiety disorders.

anxiety. Brand names include Ativan, Klonopin, and Xanax. Beta-blockers, such as Inderal, control sweating, trembling, heart conditions, and high blood pressure.

Natural stress remedies may also help you relieve stress and anxiety symptoms. Daniel K. Hall-Flavin of MayoClinic.org lists some that are being studied for effectiveness and side effects. Passionflower has proven helpful in calming the nerves and restoring sleep. Chamomile, often found in herbal tea, temporarily reduces anxiety symptoms. Lavender—taken orally or used as aromatherapy—has been known to reduce anxiety. If you plan to take these, or any other herbal supplement for stress and anxiety, consult with your doctor first. They could have adverse interactions and side effects if taken with prescription medications.

As with any substance—prescribed or natural—be sure to follow your doctor's recommendations. Be willing to work with him or her to determine which dosage or combination works best for you. You'll likely see improvements within a few weeks.

Tap into Community Resources

Another way to de-stress is to tap into community resources. Many hospitals, like Martha Jefferson Hospital in Virginia, offer free stress-management classes to community members. The city of Chandler, Arizona, has a menu of stress-busting classes through its recreation division. Teens and adults of all levels are welcome to sign up for all sorts of classes, including yoga, tai chi and meditation, and Pilates. The fees are very affordable, and the schedule runs for short intervals. Dr. Amit Sood of the Mayo Clinic offers in-person and online courses found at StressFree.org. Featured videos include "The Key to Reaching Personal Goals: Conquer Stress First!" and "Love Yourself, Like Your Pet Does."

THE LINK BETWEEN STRESS AND SOCIAL MEDIA

According to *Huffington Post's* Tyler Kingkade, "College freshmen are spending less time with friends than ever," reflecting on a declining state of mental health. This is based on the University of California, Los Angeles (UCLA) Cooperative Institutional Research Program's annual survey of "153,015 first-time, full-time students from 227 colleges and universities." For the last forty-nine years, the study has indicated a decline in emotional health. In 2014, it was at an all-time low.

Kevin Eagan, director of the UCLA program, believes emotional health is declining because students aren't taking advantage of effective coping solutions. He recognizes a link between low emotional health and an increase in social media usage.

Dr. Victor Schwartz of the Jed Foundation states, "One of the things we have seen is there is an association of depression and time spent on social media." *Huffington Post's* Kingkade points out the similarity between this observation and a University of Missouri study "linking heavy Facebook usage with feelings of envy and depression. Similar research in Austria in 2014 showed the more time someone spent on Facebook, the more they felt like they were wasting their life."

But Schwartz warns readers: "It's hard, often, to know which is the chicken and which is the egg." In other words, the survey did not clearly identify whether or not students were stressed first and went online to de-stress or if they were online first and then became stressed.

If you belong to a health management organization (HMO), you have access to special classes and workshops. One such HMO is Kaiser Permanente. This organization has services for people of all ages with emotional and behavioral problems, such as anxiety, depression, relationship issues, and drug and alcohol abuse. Nonprofit organizations, such as the National Alliance on Mental Illness (NAMI), the Anxiety and Depression Association of America, and the National Institute of Mental Health, are dedicated to your quality of life. They connect people of all ages to self-help and advocacy resources as well as local services and treatment plans.

Stressful situations are opportunities in disguise. They give you a chance to take control of your life and to choose those beliefs and activities that bring health and happiness.

Stress-Free with Spirituality

Spirituality is known by many names, such as religion, self-realization, enlightenment, transcendence, love, or the divine. It can be especially helpful for those looking for purpose and inspiration. It is often associated with prayer and meditation, both of which have been linked to improving one's positive outlook on life and immune system while decreasing stress and depression.

Believers turn to a guru, priest, rabbi, shaman, imam,

chaplain, or other such spiritual leader for help during tough times. "At a given time during a health crisis or time of acute stress, core spiritual needs will emerge and the chaplain identifies what that core spiritual need is," says Laura Dunn, MD, of EverydayHealth.com. Kelly Turner, PhD, author of *Radical Remission: Surviving Cancer Against All Odds,* shares the following:

> It's not what people believe in but whether they had a daily practice that made the difference. When you are in deep prayer or meditation, your fight-or-flight response goes off and your rest-and-repair turns on. This allows your immune system to supercharge your whole body and is incredibly healing, whether you are under stress or have an actual illness or are trying to prevent illness or stress.

CAMPUSES ALLEVIATE STRESS

College students definitely have the lion's share of stressors. They leave home, face extraordinary academic demands, foster new relationships, have wild adventures, navigate financial pressures, juggle hectic schedules, and compete to get a dream job after graduation. Because of these stressors, a third of college students feel a difficult-to-function depression, according to the National College Health Assessment. More than half experience overwhelming anxiety, while nearly 8 percent seriously consider suicide. In fact, suicide is the second leading cause of death among college students.

In response, colleges and universities have created stress-busting programs to help students extinguish stress, revive optimism, and get the support they need to forge ahead.

(contiued on the next page)

)continued from previous page)

College and high school students should take time to feed mind, body, and soul. Write some music or poetry. Dance in the kitchen. Visit a museum. Donate to a shelter.

For example, Wake Forest University in North Carolina has turned its quad into a stress-free zone. Students can read magazines, sip coffee, join games like football and Frisbee, and even tinker on an outdoor piano. Some schools, such as the University of Missouri, provide meditation training. Others, such as Kent State University in Ohio, bring in cuddly canines to help students de-stress. The University of California at Davis has a mind spa devoted to relaxation and free resources. Besides comfortable massage recliners, it offers a biofeedback program that measures breathing, body temperature, and heart rate. Students are able to let go of stress and anxiety through games and activities. The mind spa's services include free ten-minute chair massages with a massage therapist and light therapy to enhance mood and offset depression in the fall and winter months.

Seeking Support

When people need to feel less isolated and more connected, they turn to support groups. Support groups are made up of members who share a common health, relationship, or life interest. There is an understanding among them that the space in which they share is safe, confidential, and free from judgment. Support groups offer a sense of control over your life, while giving you an understanding of what to expect. You'll be able to compare notes about experiences, symptoms, advice, resources, treatments, and health care providers.

Support groups are available in person, by phone, or online. One example is DailyStrength.org. It offers health experts and

Meaningful connections help to lower rates of anxiety and depression. They also boost your self-esteem, trust, cooperation, and empathy for others.

more than five hundred communities of "people facing similar life challenges, medical conditions, and mental health issues." Topics include everything from abstinence and celibacy to break-ups and divorce.

START YOUR OWN SUPPORT GROUP

Support groups can create a welcoming environment in which others can address and overcome troubling issues. If you're so inspired—and have the time, passion, and resources—you can start your own. It will require a lot of work, but it will also be very rewarding for you and those you are trying to serve.

First, make sure you understand that while you'll be helping some, you won't be able to help everyone. You'll also want to consider the logistics, such as group size and creating a safe, respectful, and nonjudgmental atmosphere in which group members can freely share. Meetings usually last two hours and are held biweekly or monthly. They can be hosted in a school, church, or community center.

You'll also want to consider spreading the word about your group. This takes some marketing know-how. Printed fliers and newspaper ads can help, as well as running an online campaign with a website, blog, videos, and social networking sites. Be sure to add all of the important details from the who, what, and why to the when, where, and how to get involved. Finally, you'll have to be willing to speak up to maintain the mission of the group, keep the discussion on topic, and handle the situation if someone or something gets out of hand.

Support groups are facilitated by someone who is dealing with issues or is connected with the issue in some way. This includes a layperson or a professional facilitator, such as a nurse, psychologist, or social worker. Support groups can also be created by mental health clinics, nonprofit organizations, or advocacy organizations. There are thousands of support groups across the country, and while they do not replace medical care, these groups offer valuable resources that can help you reach your goals.

If you're ready to find a support group, talk with your doctor or health care provider. He or she may be able to recommend the right support group to meet your needs. If you don't have a medical professional, check in with friends and family or go online to find a local or national organization dedicated to your condition.

In this stress-filled world, you'll be challenged to stay on top of your mental and physical health. You'll be challenged to plan every moment of your life with one activity after the next. But you make the time to relax, refresh, and rejuvenate. Learn to listen to your body, recognize your stressors, and make the most of online and in-person resources. Now's the time to take control of your life and defeat stress and anxiety for good!

Glossary

ABSTINENCE The decision to refrain from indulging in an activity, such as eating, drinking, and participating in sexual activity.

AFFIRMATIOn A statement of positivity and encouragement.

AROMATHERAPY The practice of using natural oils to improve health and well-being.

BOTTLE ROT Severe tooth decay in infants and young children caused by sugary beverages and poor dental hygiene.

CELIBACY A state of being unmarried or refraining from sexual activity.

DILATE To widen or grow larger.

ENDOCRINE SYSTEM Glands and related parts that generate endocrine solutions, such as hormones.

ENDOCRINOLOGIST A doctor who treats hormone imbalances from glands in the endocrine system.

ENDORPHIN A group of substances in the nervous system that regulate the body's response to stimuli.

EXHALATION The act of releasing one's breath.

GENETICS A branch of biology that addresses the physical and mental qualities shared between parent and child.

GLUCOSE A natural sugar found in the blood.

GROUP THERAPY A type of therapy in which a group is overseen by a trained professional and patients discuss a particular condition and share insight.

HORMONE A chemical made by the body to start a reaction in the body.

HYPNOSIS A trancelike state of altered consciousness.

HYPOTHALAMUS A part of the brain that manufactures hormones.

INHALATION The act of breathing inwardly.

MEDITATE To take the time to quiet the mind using relaxation techniques, breathing exercises, affirmations, or prayer.

METABOLISM The body's chemical process for using food and water to manufacture the energy to function.

PROCRASTINATE To put off a priority until another time.

PSYCHIATRIST A medical professional who studies mental, emotional, or behavioral disorders.

PSYCHOLOGIST A trained professional who studies the science of the mind and behavior.

SUBSTANCE ABUSE The misuse of alcohol and drugs that leads to harmful or hazardous effects.

Anxiety and Depression Association of America (ADAA)
8701 Georgia Avenue, Suite 412
Silver Spring, MD 20910
(240) 485-1001
Website: http://www.adaa.org
Using education, practice, and research, the ADAA promotes
early diagnosis, treatment, and cures for those suffering
from anxiety, depression, PTSD, OCD, and related
disorders.

Childhelp National Child Abuse Hotline
4350 E. Camelback Road, Building F250
Phoenix, AZ 85018
(800) 4-A-CHILD (422-4453)
Website: http://www.childhelpusa.org
Since 1982, the Childhelp National Child Abuse Hotline has
been committed to the prevention of child abuse in the
United States, its territories, and Canada. Professional
crisis counselors work with interpreters to provide help to
youngsters and distressed parents in 170 languages.

Crisis Call Center
P.O. Box 8016
Reno, NV 89507
(800) 273-8255 or text "ANSWER" to 839863
Website: http://crisiscallcenter.org/crisisservices.html
Crisis Call Center's twenty-four-hour crisis line provides safe,

nonjudgmental, and free emotional support for those seeking help, resources, and crisis intervention. Topics include substance abuse, domestic violence, and child/elder abuse or neglect.

The Jed Foundation
1140 Broadway, Suite 803
New York, NY 10001
(212) 647-7544
Website: https://www.jedfoundation.org
The Jed Foundation works to protect the emotional health of America's twenty-one million college students. Its award-winning programs advocate for mental health and prevent suicide.

Kids Help Phone
Alberta and Northwest Territories
4331 Manhattan Road SE
Calgary, Alberta T2G 4B1
Canada
(866) 297-4101

British Columbia and the Yukon
Suite 570, 789 West Pender Street
Vancouver, BC V6C 1H2
Canada
(844) 849-4551

Ontario and National
300-439 University Avenue
Toronto, ON M5G 1Y8

Canada
(800) 268-3062

(800) 668-6868
Website: http://kidshelpphone.ca/Teens
Kids Help Phone offers twenty-four-hour toll-free and bilingual (French and English) phone and web counseling and
a referral service for Canada's youth. Its services are anonymous and confidential.

loveisrespect, National Teen Dating Abuse Helpline
P.O. Box 161810
Austin, TX 78716
(866) 331-9474
Text "loveis" to 22522*
Website: http://www.loveisrespect.org
Highly trained peer advocates at loveisrespect offer free and
confidential support for the prevention and termination
of relationship abuse. It is a partnership of the National
Domestic Violence Hotline and Break the Cycle.

Mental Health Association (MHA)
2000 N. Beauregard Street, 6th Floor
Alexandria, VA 22311
(800) 969-6642
Website: http://www.nmha.org
Since 1909, the MHA has promoted mental health with
prevention, early detection, intervention, and treatment
services.

National Alliance on Mental Illness (NAMI)
N. Fairfax Drive, Suite 100
Arlington, VA 22203
(703) 524-7600
Website: http://www.nami.org
Since 1979, NAMI has dedicated its efforts to the eradication
of mental illnesses and to the life improvement of those
who are affected by these diseases. Today, it has hundreds
of local affiliates, state organizations, and volunteers who
raise awareness and provide education and support.

Rape, Abuse & Incest National Network (RAINN)
1220 L Street NW, Suite 505
Washington, DC 20005
(800) 656-HOPE (4673)
Website: http://www.rainn.org
RAINN created and runs the National Sexual Assault Hotline
in partnership with more than 1,100 rape crisis centers
across the United States. It helps victims, advocates for
prevention of sexual violence, and works to bring rapists
to justice.

TEEN LINE
P.O. Box 48750
Los Angeles, CA 90048
(310) 855-HOPE (4673)
(800) TLC-TEEN (852-8336) (toll-free in California only)
Website: https://teenlineonline.org
TEEN LINE addresses various issues teens face today with a
blog, message board, downloads, videos, teen line, and
online Youth Yellow Pages.

Trans Lifeline
United States: (877) 565-8860
Canada: (877) 330-6366
Website: http://www.translifeline.org
Trans Lifeline is a nonprofit group dedicated to the well-
    being of transgender people. Its twenty-four-hour,
    seven-days-a-week hotline is staffed by transgender
    volunteers who are educated in the challenges facing
    transgender people.

Websites
Because of the changing nature of Internet links, Rosen
    Publishing has developed an online list of websites
    related to the subject of this book. This site is updated
    regularly. Please use this link to access the list:
http://www.rosenlinks.com/ESS/Stress

For Further Reading

Carnegie, Dale. *How to Stop Worrying and Start Living*. New York, NY: Simon & Schuster, Inc., 2010.

Collins-Donnelly, Kate. *Starving the Anxiety Gremlin: A Cognitive Behavioural Therapy Workbook on Anxiety Management for Young People*. Philadelphia, PA: Jessica Kingsley Publishers, 2013.

Nhat Hanh, Thich. *A Handful of Quiet: Happiness in Four Pebbles*. Berkeley, CA: Plum Blossom Books, 2012.

Nhat Hanh, Thich. *Silence: The Power of Quiet in a World Full of Noise*. New York, NY: HarperOne, 2015.

Purcell, Mark C., and Jason R Murphy. *Mindfulness for Teen Anger: A Workbook to Overcome Anger and Aggression Using MBSR and DBT Skills*. Oakland, CA: Instant Help Books, 2014.

Shannon, Jennifer. *The Shyness and Social Anxiety Workbook for Teens: CBT and ACT Skills to Help You Build Social Confidence*. Oakland, CA: Instant Help Books, 2012.

Sood, Amit. *Mayo Clinic Guide to Stress-Free Living*. Boston, MA: Mayo Foundation for Medical Education and Research, 2013.

Tompkins, Michael A., and Katherine A. Martinez. *My Anxious Mind: A Teen's Guide to Managing Anxiety and Panic*. Washington, DC: Magination Press, 2010.

Van Dijk, Sheri. *Don't Let Your Emotions Run Your Life for Teens: Dialectical Behavior Therapy Skills for Helping You Manage Mood Swings, Control Angry Outbursts, and Get Along with Others*. Oakland, CA: Instant Help Books, 2011.

Van Dijk, Sheri. *Relationship Skills 101 for Teens: Your Guide to Dealing with Daily Drama, Stress, and Difficult Emotions Using DBT.* Oakland, CA: Instant Help Books, 2015.

Vo, Dzung X., MD, FAAP. *The Mindful Teen: Powerful Skills to Help You Handle Stress One Moment at a Time.* Oakland, CA: Instant Help Books, 2015.

Willard, Christopher. *Mindfulness for Teen Anxiety: A Workbook for Overcoming Anxiety at Home, at School, and Everywhere Else.* Oakland, CA: Instant Help Books, 2014.

Bibliography

Anxiety and Depression Association of America. "Start a Support Group." Retrieved April 29, 2015 (http://www.adaa.org/finding-help/getting-support/support-groups/start-support-group).

Choosemyplate.gov. "Welcome to the Five Food Groups." Retrieved April 4, 2015 (http://www.choosemyplate.gov/food-groups).

City of Chandler, AZ. "Recreation Programs & Activities." Retrieved April 25, 2015 (http://www.chandleraz.gov/default.aspx?pageid=78f).

Dowell, Ben. "Prince William—Fatherhood Has Made Me More Emotionally in Tune with the World." RadioTimes. Retrieved April 18, 2015 (http://www.radiotimes.com/news/2013-09-09).

Goodman, Lizzy. "Taylor Swift: Whole Lotta Love." Elle.com. Retrieved May 3, 2015. (http://www.elle.com/culture/celebrities/g5656/taylor-swift-quotes-fashion-photos/?slide=3).

Gregoire, Carolyn. "Gymnast McKayla Maroney Talks Life Post-Olympics, Becoming a Meme & How She De-Stresses." Huffington Post. Retrieved April 18, 2015 (http://www.huffingtonpost.com/2013/03/01/mckayla-maroney-interview_n_2776397.html).

Hall-Flavin, Daniel K. "Can Chronic Stress Cause Depression?" Mayo Clinic. Retrieved May 3, 2015. (http://www.mayoclinic.org/healthy-lifestyle/stress-management).

Hall-Flavin, Daniel K. "Is There an Effective Herbal Treatment for Anxiety?" Mayo Clinic. Retrieved April 22, 2015 (http://www.mayoclinic.org/diseases-conditions/ generalized-anxiety-disorder).

HelpGuide.org. "Therapy for Anxiety Disorders." Retrieved May 3, 2015 (http://www.helpguide.org/articles/anxiety/ therapy-for-anxiety-disorders.htm).

Howard, Beth. "Schools Take on Stress." USnews.com. Retrieved April 25, 2015 (http://www.usnews.com/news/ college-of-tomorrow/articles/2014/09/22).

Huffington Post. "Goldie Hawn Shares Her De-Stress Tips with Katie Couric." February 4, 2013. Retrieved April 5, 2015 (http://www.huffingtonpost.com/2013/02/04/ goldie-hawn-de-stress-tips-katie-couric).

Huffington Post. "How Celebrities Relax: 11 Young Stars on How They Unwind & De-Stress." Retrieved April 15, 2015 (http://www.huffingtonpost.com/2013/02/25/how -celebrities-relax-11-_n_2759340.html).

Huffington Post. "Jennifer Lawrence Reveals She Battled Anxiety Growing Up: 'I Felt Worthless.'" Retrieved April 21, 2015 (http://www.huffingtonpost.com/2013/11/18/ jennifer-lawrence-anxiety-battle_n_4296600.html).

Huffington Post. "Stress Relief Tips: 8 Quick & Easy Online Tension-Busters." Retrieved April 5, 2015 (http://www .huffingtonpost.com/2013/03/14/stress-relief-tips-10 -qui_n_2868236.html).

Jayson, Sharon. "Teens Feeling Stressed, and Many Not Managing It Well." *USA Today*. Retrieved April 10, 2015 (http://www.usatoday.com/story/news/nation/2014/02/11/ stress-teens-psychological/5266739).

Johnson, Zach. "Video: Vinny Guadagnino: What It's Like to Have Clinical Anxiety." *US Weekly*. Retrieved May 3, 2015. (http://www.usmagazine.com/celebrity-news/news).

Kaiser Permanente. "Caring for the Whole You." Retrieved

April 25, 2015. (https://healthy.kaiserpermanente.org).

Kelly, Andy. "PC's Most Relaxing Games." PC Gamer. Retrieved May 3, 2015 (http://www.pcgamer.com/the-most-relaxing-games-on-pc).

KidsHealth.org. "Stress." Reviewed by D'Arcy Lyness. Retrieved April 10, 2015 (http://m.kidshealth.org/teen/your_mind/emotions/stress.html).

Kingkade, Tyler. "College Freshmen Are More Depressed and Alone Than Ever." *Huffington Post*. Retrieved April 25, 2015 (http://www.huffingtonpost.com/2015/02/05/college-students-depressed-ucla_n_6624012.html).

Levin, Rebecca. "Miley Cyrus Relationship Anxiety." Anxiety.org. Retrieved April 21, 2015 (https://www.anxiety.org/miley-cyrus-relationship-anxiety).

Lundgren, Tammie. Interview by Erin Staley. Murrieta, CA, April 19, 2015.

Mann, Denise. "6 Ways Spirituality Can Make You Healthier." Everyday Health. Retrieved April 27, 2015. (http://www.everydayhealth.com/pictures/ways-spirituality-can-make-you-healthier/#01).

Mayo Clinic Staff. "Panic Attacks and Panic Disorder." Mayo Clinic. Retrieved May 3, 2015 (http://www.mayoclinic.org/diseases-conditions/panic-attacks/basics/definition/con-20020825).

Mayo Clinic Staff. "Stress Relief from Laughter? It's No Joke." Mayo Clinic. Retrieved April 5, 2015 (http://www.mayoclinic.org/healthy-lifestyle/stress-management/in-depth/stress-relief).

Mayo Clinic Staff. "Support Groups: Make Connections, Get Help." Mayo Clinic. Retrieved March 21, 2015 (http://www.mayoclinic.org/healthy-living/stress-management/in-depth/support-groups).

Mckaylamaroney.com. "McKayla Maroney." Retrieved April 18, 2015 (http://www.mckaylamaroney.com/bio).

Msn.com. "18 Celebrity Tips on Dealing with Stress." Retrieved April 4, 2015 (http://www.msn.com/en-us/ health/wellness/18-celebrity-tips-on-dealing-with-stress).

National Institute of Mental Health. "Anxiety Disorders." Retrieved April 29, 2015 (http://www.nimh.nih.gov/ health/topics/anxiety-disorders/index.shtml).

National Sleep Foundation. "Sleep Drive and Your Body Clock." Retrieved April 8, 2015 (http://sleepfoundation. org/sleep-topics/ sleep-drive-and-your-body-clock?page=0%2C0).

Palmiter, David J., and Dawn Wilson. "Teens and Stress: How to Keep Stress in Check." American Psychological Association. Retrieved April 10, 2015 (http://www.apa. org/helpcenter/stress-teens.aspx).

Ramaswamy, Chitra. "Interview: Viggo Mortensen Is Lord of All Things." The Scotsman. Retrieved April 5, 2015 (http:// www.scotsman.com/what-s-on/film).

Resilient Living. "Resilient Living." Retrieved April 25, 2015 (http://stressfree.org).

Saldi, Sara R. "Therapy Dogs Help Relieve Exam Stress." UB Reporter. Retrieved April 20, 2015 (http://www.buffalo. edu/ubreporter/campus/campus-host-page.host.html/ content).

Scott, Jennifer Acosta. "Famous People Get Anxious, Too." Everyday Health. Retrieved May 3, 2015 (http://www. everydayhealth.com/anxiety-pictures/celebrities-with- anxiety-disorders.aspx#08).

Takeda, Allison. "Jennifer Lawrence Reveals She Had Therapy for Social Anxiety: 'I Felt Worthless.'" *US Weekly*.

Retrieved May 3, 2015 (http://www.usmagazine.com/
celebrity-news/news).

UC Davis Student Affairs. "The Mind Spa." Retrieved May 2,
2015 (https://shcs.ucdavis.edu/services/mindspa.html).

UN Volunteers. "UN Youth Volunteers: Who We're Looking
For." Retrieved April 28, 2015 (http://www.unv.org/what-
we-do/youth/un-youth-volunteers-who-were-looking-for
.html).

Vine, Richard. "Why Buffaloes and Crickets Help Us Relax."
Guardian. Retrieved April 10, 2015 (http://www
.theguardian.com/lifeandstyle/shortcuts/2013/sep/10).

Watson, Stephanie. "Volunteering May Be Good for Body
and Mind." Harvard Health Publications: Harvard Medical
School. Retrieved April 27, 2015 (http://www.health
.harvard.edu/blog).

WebMD.com. "Foods That Help Tame Stress." Reviewed by
Kathleen M. Zelman. Retrieved April 16, 2014 (http://
www.webmd.com/diet/ss/slideshow-diet-for-stress
-management).

YouTube. "National Geographic: The Science of Stress."
Posted by "The TV Re-Do Guy," August 19, 2013. (http://
youtu.be/ZyBsy5SQxqU).

Index

About the Author

After running a successful dance program for more than a decade, Erin Staley took her stories from the stage to the page as a writer. Forever a student of the human condition, Staley fostered a passion for the inner workings of the mind and body. Today, she writes as an international recruitment creative copywriter for the University of California, Riverside. This is the tenth book Staley has authored for Rosen Publishing.

Photo Credits

Cover © iStockphoto.com/Fertnig; p. 5 Diego Cervo/Shutterstock.com; pp. 6, 33 wavebreakmedia/Shutterstock.com; p. 9 LaRae Lundgren; p. 12 Chelsea Lauren/WireImage/Getty Images; p. 13 Dean Mouhtaropoulos/Getty Images; p. 16 Minerva Studio/Shutterstock.com; p. 18 kobrin_photo/iStock/Thinkstock; p. 20 Andrea Morini/Photodisc/Thinkstock; p. 24 Creatista/Shutterstock.com; p. 25 moodboard/Thinkstock; p. 28 Ezra Shaw/Digital Vision/Thinkstock; p. 30 © iStockphoto.com/SilviaJansen; p. 34 Andrea Raffin/Shutterstock.com; p. 36 luminaimages/Shutterstock.com; p. 39 Alexander Raths/Shutterstock.com; p. 42 gary yim/Shutterstock.com; p. 44 PathDoc/Shutterstock.com; p. 45 bikeriderlondon/Shutterstock.com; back cover and interior pages background pattern ONiONA/Shutterstock.com

Designer: Nicole Russo; Editor: Heather Niver;

The American Newsboy

by Michael Burgan

Content Adviser: Melodie Andrews, Ph.D.,
Associate Professor of Early American History,
Minnesota State University, Mankato

Reading Adviser: Rosemary G. Palmer, Ph.D.,
Department of Literacy, College of Education,
Boise State University

Compass Point Books ✦ Minneapolis, Minnesota

Compass Point Books
3109 West 50th Street, #115
Minneapolis, MN 55410

Visit Compass Point Books on the Internet at *www.compasspointbooks.com*
or e-mail your request to *custserv@compasspointbooks.com*

On the cover: Newsboys on the steps of a bank in Jersey City, New Jersey

Photographs Corbis, cover, 14; Prints Old and Rare, back cover (far left); Library of Congress,
back cover, 6, 7, 13, 15, 16, 17, 23, 35, 36; Bettmann/Corbis, 5, 9, 11, 19, 27, 39; Corbis, 14;
Getty Images Inc., 20; Picture Collection, The Branch Libraries, The New York Public Library,
Astor, Lenox and Tilden Foundations, 21, 22; Kansas State Historical Society, 25; Underwood
and Underwood/Corbis, 26, 30; The Granger Collection, New York, 28, 32; Lewis W. Hine/
George Eastman House/Getty Images, 37; Timothy Pratt, 40.

Editor: Sue Vander Hook
Page Production: Blue Tricycle, Bobbie Nuytten
Photo Researcher: Lori Bye
Cartographer: XNR Productions, Inc.
Library Consultant: Kathleen Baxter

Creative Director: Keith Griffin
Editorial Director: Carol Jones
Managing Editor: Catherine Neitge

Library of Congress Cataloging-in-Publication Data
Burgan, Michael
  The American newsboy / by Michael Burgan.
    p. cm.—(We the people)
Includes bibliographical references and index.
  ISBN-13: 978-0-7565-2458-6 (library binding)
  ISBN-10: 0-7565-2458-X (library binding)
1. Paperboys—United States—History—Juvenile literature. 2. Children with social
disabilities—United States—History—Juvenile literature. 3. Poor children—United States—
History—Juvenile literature. 4. Newspaper carriers—United States—History—Juvenile
literature. I. Title. II. (Series).
  HD8039.N422U635 2007
  331.3'18—dc22   2006027085

TABLE OF CONTENTS

BRINGING NEWS TO THE STREETS

"Extra! Extra! Read all about it!" That was a famous cry of American newsboys. They made a living walking the streets, doing what they could to get busy people to stop and buy their newspapers.

On September 4, 1833, 10-year-old Bernard Flaherty took to the streets. Standing on a street corner, he shouted at passersby to buy a copy of the *New York Sun*, a brand-new newspaper. Unlike other New York City papers, the *Sun* cost only a penny and was sold on the streets, not in stores or by subscription. That day, Bernard made history as the first known American newsboy.

His workplace was the city where horse-drawn wagons rattled along dirt streets and thousands of people scurried to work. New York was the largest city in the United States, with more than 200,000 people. It was the country's banking center and the site of a major port.

Until 1919, it was legal for children of any age to work and not attend school.

New York City in the late 1800s at the corner of Fifth Avenue and 46th Street

In years to come, more newsboys—and a few news-girls—would stand on the street corners of New York and other major U.S. cities. They would shout out the latest headlines to persuade people to buy newspapers. The money they made would help them survive.

By the end of the 1800s, Americans across the country knew about newsboys. Books and magazines printed pictures of them, and the boys appeared as characters in books. Decades later, movies would feature newsboys, or "news-ies," as they were called. They became famous, but newsboys' real lives were not easy.

NEWSPAPERS AND THE BOYS WHO SOLD THEM

The first newspaper appeared in America in 1690.

During the 1700s, most papers were published weekly.

They included advertisements, news about ships arriving

The Pennsylvania Journal and Weekly Advertiser *was printed in the 1760s when England still ruled the 13 colonies.*

7

from England, and letters from readers describing daily experiences. Sometimes newspapers reprinted articles that had already been published in other papers.

Readers usually bought newspapers at the post office or a local store. Newspaper publishers also sold subscriptions, which was a way to get people to pay in advance to have their papers delivered. As a teen, Benjamin Franklin told how he was "employed to carry the papers thro' the streets to the customers." Franklin went on to become a great scientist and U.S. government official.

By the 1760s, a few publishers were using young boys to sell newspapers on the streets. One such New York paper was the *Constitutional Courant.* It was not really a newspaper, however, but one long article. At that time, colonists were writing about Great Britain, which controlled the 13 colonies that would later become the United States of America. The articles were meant to stir up anger toward the British.

After the colonies won their independence from

England in 1783, more newspapers slowly appeared. They published articles mostly about politics and business. In large cities, daily papers became common, but they cost too much for the average working person. In 1830, a typical New York paper cost 6 cents. At the time, most

In the late 1800s, newsboys sold newspapers in Chicago, Illinois, for just 3 cents each.

people earned less than $1 a day.

A printer named Benjamin Henry Day decided to publish a newspaper that cost only a penny—a price more people could afford. He wanted his newspaper to have articles about average people and events of the city. He called it the *New York Sun*. Day published his first issue of the *Sun* on September 3, 1833. In it, he placed an ad seeking "a number of steady men" who wanted work "vending this paper."

The next day, 10-year-old Bernard Flaherty showed up looking for a job. The following day, this young Irish-born immigrant was on the streets of New York City selling the *Sun*. Most New York newsboys who followed him were also young immigrants.

Day liked the idea of using boys instead of men to sell his papers. It was one way he could save money, since men demanded higher salaries. Boys were already selling papers in London. A 2-cent newspaper that failed earlier in the year had used newsboys. But Day got credit for hiring the first American newsboy.

At first, Flaherty had trouble selling his papers. The *Sun* was smaller than other newspapers, and Flaherty had a

10

The New York Sun *was published from 1833 to 1919, when it merged with the* New York Herald.

high, squeaky voice. People were startled to hear him shouting in their ears. But the *Sun*—and newsboys—soon became common sights in New York City.

A NEWSBOY'S LIFE

Each morning, newsboys bought newspapers that were printed during the night. Benjamin Day charged his newsboys 67 cents for 100 copies of the *New York Sun*. If a boy sold all 100 papers, he would make 33 cents. Newsboys could also buy papers on credit, or a promise to pay later. Then the cost went up to 75 cents. If the boys didn't sell all their papers, they couldn't return them. So they worked hard to sell them all. They shouted out headlines, trying to attract buyers to their newspapers, or sheets, as they were sometimes called. In some cities, a newsboy's work was called "hustling the sheets."

The *Sun* was successful, and soon other New York publishers printed penny papers. They also used newsboys to sell them. Most publishers were in southern Manhattan in New York City in an area called Newspaper Row or Printing House Square.

Early in the morning, boys gathered at Newspaper

Newspaper Row, former publishing headquarters of the World *(left), the* Tribune, *and the* Times *in the Manhattan area of New York City in 1906*

Row, waiting for bundles of newspapers. They folded their papers, put them in bags, and headed to crowded streets throughout the city. Some boys also sold newspapers printed in the afternoon. They stayed on the streets into the evening to sell these editions.

Newsboys worked long hours for one reason—they needed money. If they lived with their families, they

13

brought home what they earned. But more often than not, they were orphans, and they used their earnings to buy food and survive as best they could. Many of them lived on the streets, which was not uncommon for children at the time. One U.S. newspaper reported that the homeless children of New York had a "semi-savage and wandering mode of life."

Homeless newsboys often slept in the stairwells of newspaper buildings so they could pick up their papers first thing in the morning.

Newsboys were all ages, some as young as 6 years old.

In the 1850s, some Americans concerned about newsboys and other orphans tried to improve life for these children.

15

HELPING OUT

Charles Loring Brace was one of the first people who tried to help newsboys. After studying to become a minister, Brace came to New York in 1848. He saw how many people—adults and children—were living in terrible poverty. In the 1800s, the United States was growing quickly as poor immigrants flooded into the country. From 1820 to 1850, the nation's population grew from less than 10 million people to more than 23 million. By 1900, almost 76 million people lived in the United States.

Charles Loring Brace (1826–1890)

16

The father of a family often couldn't find a job, and the mother and children would work for as little as $1.50 to $2 a week.

More than 10 million of them were immigrants.

People usually looked for work in large cities. At times, they took jobs that didn't pay well, and other times, they found no jobs at all. Some children worked to help their families. Others left home because they knew their parents couldn't afford to take care of them.

In Manhattan, some of the poorest people lived in a neighborhood called Five Points. Apartment buildings there were crowded, and homes didn't have running water

17

or bathrooms. Diseases were common and often were deadly. Parents sometimes died, and children were left behind as orphans.

Men found it difficult to find and keep a job. To escape from their hard lives, fathers—and occasionally mothers—sometimes drank too much alcohol. Children left home rather than face poverty or a drunken parent. An 1849 police report stated that 3,000 children lived on their own in the streets of Manhattan. Some of these streets where they lived and slept had nicknames such as Misery Row and Poverty Lane.

Brace wrote that newsboys "slept one winter in the iron tube of the bridge at Harlem; two others made their bed in a burned-out safe in Wall Street." But Brace didn't just study the problem; he also tried to help newsboys and other homeless youngsters in New York.

At first, he and other reformers rounded up newsboys and young members of street gangs and brought them to religious meetings. The boys, however, were not always

Newsboys found anyplace to sleep, such as outside a New York church.

open to what was said. At some meetings, fights broke out among gang members.

    In 1853, Brace and some of his friends started the Children's Aid Society to help needy children. Both boys and girls came to the organization. Among the boys were newsboys and bootblacks, people who shined shoes for money. The girls who came were often orphans who earned

A Londoner was one of many newsboys around the world.

pennies selling candy or apples. Brace wrote that the children came to the Society "telling their simple stories of suffering, and loneliness … until our hearts became sick."

In 1854, the Children's Aid Society opened the
Newsboys' Lodging House. Brace convinced the owners of

the *New York Sun* to donate space in their building for the homeless shelter. The house was the first of its kind in the United States.

Boys—most of them news-boys—paid 6 cents a night to sleep in a clean bed and take a bath. For another 4 cents, they got a hot meal. Boys with worn clothes or shoes received new ones. Brace wanted the boys to help pay the cost of running the home. He also wanted to teach them how to handle the money they earned selling papers. Over time, the home set up a bank for the boys so they could save money instead of spending it on foolish things.

The house had about

The Newsboys' Lodging House was in the New York Sun *building.*

21

40 beds, a bathroom, and a large dining room. Boys who caused trouble were thrown back out onto the streets. Newsboys learned it was easier to behave than to find a new place to sleep. As one newsboy said to another, "I say, Jim, this is rather better than bumming, eh?"

Since the boys had no time during the day to go to school, the home held classes in the evening. Most of the boys weren't interested in learning to read or write, until the home's director convinced them they could make more

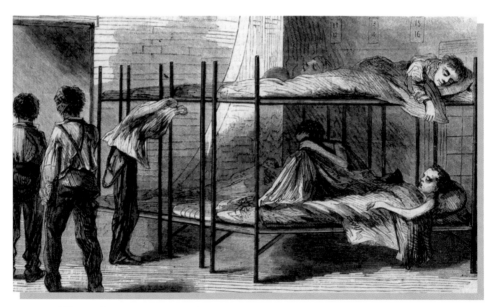

The Lodging House provided beds for orphaned newsboys for a few cents a day.

Homeless boys shared Christmas dinner together.

money with an education.

One of the students was an intelligent boy named Johnny Morrow. Once a thief, he now sold matchsticks. But his education at the home would prepare him to one day attend a school in Connecticut, where he would study religion. Although Morrow died in 1861 at the age of 20, he left a written account of the hard life of newsboys. In 1860, he wrote *A Voice from the Newsboys*, a book about his time at the home and how the Children's Aid Society helped him. Although one modern historian doesn't believe it is entirely true, the book does describe what newsboys and orphans faced.

Because living on city streets was dangerous and unhealthy, Brace and the Children's Aid Society worked to find families for newsboys and other orphans. The best thing for them, Brace believed, was to "send them away to kind Christian homes in the country." After all, farm families would welcome the children because they could help out with chores. In 1854, the first trains filled with orphans left New York City. Over the next 75 years, about 200,000 children boarded what came to be called orphan trains and traveled West to new families and homes.

The Roman Catholic Church also helped newsboys. In 1871, Father John Christopher Drumgoole founded the St. Vincent's Home for Homeless Newsboys, located in an old warehouse near Newspaper Row. Like Brace's home, it took in newsboys and other orphans. Drumgoole offered classes in woodworking, shoemaking, and baking. Later, in 1906, a priest named Peter Dunne started a home for newsboys in St. Louis, Missouri.

The children who boarded orphan trains had no idea where they were going.

Businesses also began helping newsboys. Some of them took the boys out for picnics or gave them clothing. In Toledo, Ohio, business leaders formed a Newsboys Association, which later formed its own marching band.

Newspaper publishers also did a few things to help their own newsboys. They provided a special free broadsheet the boys could give their customers on New Year's Day. The readers were supposed to give the boys a gift in

Actress Lois Moran and co-worker Richard Imess gave Thanksgiving baskets to newsboys who lived in Brace's home for boys.

return. By the late 1800s, some newspapers had started educational classes for newsboys, although by then most states required children under 12 to attend school.

NEWSBOYS IN PRINT

The lives and experiences of newsboys became a favorite subject for some writers. In 1872, one author described newsboys as "ragged and dirty." He complained, "They surround you on the sidewalk and almost force you to buy their papers." But other writers thought newsboys were basically good.

One of the most famous of these writers was Horatio Alger, who wrote about newsboys and orphans of New York. In his first book, *Ragged Dick*, and in another, *Nelson the Newsboy*, he described the boys as hardworking, well-meaning children. In *Cast Upon the Breakers*, he

Horatio Alger wrote more than 100 books about poor boys who became successful.

27

ROUGH AND READY

Horatio Alger's books in the Ragged Dick series featured young, hardworking newsboys.

wrote, "Many of them were fun loving and even mischievous, but scarcely any were really bad." All they needed, he thought, was a chance to succeed.

For a while, Alger lived at the Newsboys' Lodging House to learn more about newsboys. The house became the setting for some of his stories. Alger's books were later called rags-to-riches stories, since some of his characters managed to get good jobs and rise above their lives of poverty. Alger hoped leaders in business and government would see the value in helping these boys improve their lives.

Stories about newsboys were common throughout the 1800s. In 1891, Richard Harding Davis, a reporter for the *New York Sun*, published his fiction book, *Gallegher and Other Stories*. Gallegher, the main character, was a newsboy who sometimes solved crimes. In the 1900s, more authors wrote about newsboys.

Harry E. Burroughs, a newsboy himself, wrote about his own experiences. After leaving Russia in 1903, he worked as a newsboy in Boston, Massachusetts. At first, he didn't know that each newsboy had his own special corner where he sold papers. He wrote, "I was 'cutting out' another boy. … I knew he was mad, but I did not know why. Finally he hit me, and I hit back, and we rolled around in the gutter until someone separated us."

Burroughs became a true example of a rags-to-riches story. Unlike most newsboys, Burroughs went to school and also sold newspapers every day. Later, he became a successful lawyer. In 1927, he started the Burroughs Newsboys

Boys at the Burroughs Newsboys Foundation learned how to box
with air-inflated gloves.

Foundation in Boston to help newsboys. Boys were given
the chance to play sports, study art, and save money. The
foundation's motto was "Strive. Serve. Save. Study."

FIGHTING FOR BETTER PAY

The Children's Aid Society and concerned Americans were helping newsboys. But sometimes the boys had to act on their own to improve their lives—they had to demand better pay.

In 1898, New York newspapers were publishing articles about the Spanish-American War. Americans were eager for the news, and newspaper sales rose. Then newspaper companies increased their prices, and newsboys had to pay more for their papers.

After the United States defeated Spain and the war ended, interest in newspapers fell and sales declined. However, publishers didn't lower the cost of papers. Newsboys were still paying a high price and finding it harder to sell papers. At times, they were lucky to make 40 cents a day.

In July 1899, newsboys for the *Evening World* and the *Evening Herald* decided to go on strike. During a

31

The daily routine of hustling newspapers came to a halt when thousands of newsboys went on strike in 1899.

strike, workers refuse to work in order to convince their bosses to give them more money or improve their working conditions. Several thousand newsboys were refusing to sell newspapers.

Other newspaper publishers eagerly wrote about the strike—they were glad their competition might lose money because their newsboys wouldn't work. Newsboys for other papers tried to sell the *Evening World* and the *Evening Herald*. But striking newsboys beat them up or ran them off. The strikers wanted to make sure their two newspaper companies lost money.

The leader of the newsboy strike was Kid Blink, so called because he was blind in one eye. The *New York Tribune* reported what Kid Blink told the strikers, "Dis is de time when we'se got to stick together like glue."

Newsboys in nearby Jersey City, New Jersey, also joined the strike. Later, other newsboys went on strike in Chicago, Illinois; Boston, Massachusetts; and Pittsburgh, Pennsylvania. The New York publishers and the newsboys

New York City and Boston were popular places for newsboys to work.

finally reached a deal. The companies wouldn't lower the cost of newspapers, but they would buy back any papers the boys didn't sell. Then the newsboys went back to work.

34

END OF THE AMERICAN NEWSBOY

During the early 1900s, newsboys were still common on U.S. city streets. Some were as young as 6 years old. Most had their own corner where they worked. In Boston, if a boy wanted to leave the business, he sold the right to work on his corner to another boy.

Most newsboys had regular customers who passed their corner every day and bought a newspaper. The boys got to know the people in their neighborhood. During the 1920s, President Calvin Coolidge described the boys:

Calvin Coolidge was president of the United States from 1923 to 1929.

35

"Newsboys know all and see all."

Reformers still wanted to improve life for newsboys. One reformer named Felix Adler described the poor lives of newsboys: "They are out at all hours of the night and day, exposed to the most inclement weather. ... By the time they have reached their fourteenth year they are worn out."

In 1904, Adler and other reformers founded the National Child Labor Committee. The committee worked to set minimum age requirements for employees and limit the number of hours children could work. Other reformers called for stronger education laws so children

Felix Adler spent most of his life helping disadvantaged people.

would have to spend more years in school.

In 1919, one group of reformers said children under 16 should not be allowed to sell papers. They feared that young boys were being exposed to criminals and bad habits

A group of newsboys and shoeshine boys gambled on the sidewalk.

such as gambling, smoking, and drinking. One newspaper official, however, argued that selling papers helped boys succeed. He said they were "bright, capable, and intelligent fellows, who will eventually become America's best business men, because of the training they receive." And some of the boys did succeed.

In 1938, the U.S. government passed the first national laws to limit child labor. For most jobs, children would have to be at least 16 years old. However, newspaper publishers convinced the government not to set age limits for newsboys. They called them "little merchants" who actually didn't work for the newspaper companies. They claimed the boys were their own bosses.

Although the law allowed newsboys to stay on the streets, in time their numbers decreased. After World War II ended in 1945, many American families began moving out of the cities and into suburban areas that were just starting to grow. More people paid for papers to be delivered to their homes instead of buying them on the streets.

In 1953, a newspaper boy scanned through a daily edition of the newspaper before making his deliveries on his bicycle.

Newsboys were now called carriers, and they threw papers onto people's porches from their bicycles. Newspaper companies also set up boxes on city street corners so customers

In 1895, William L. Brown, who had worked in newspapers, erected a statue in Great Barrington, Massachusetts, as a tribute to all newsboys.

could insert a coin and take out a paper. Using a box was cheaper than paying a newsboy.

Throughout the 1900s and early 2000s, the newspaper industry continued to change. Today, only about half of adult Americans read a paper every day. The number of daily papers fell from about 1,750 in 1980 to fewer than 1,460 today. By 2006, more than 50 million people were relying on the Internet for their news.

Publishers have also changed how they deliver newspapers. As early as 3 A.M.—a time too early for most children and teens—newspapers are ready to be picked up. Since 1908, the number of young carriers has fallen from more than 800,000 to less than 200,000. Meanwhile, more adults have become carriers.

All these changes led to the end of the newsboy. But their struggles, hard work, and determination have not been forgotten. The American newsboy remains an important part of U.S. history.

GLOSSARY

credit—a loan of goods or money with a promise to repay

immigrant—someone who moves from one country to live permanently in another

motto—a short saying that describes the goal of a person or group

orphans—children whose parents have died

reformers—people who try to improve life for others

strike—when workers refuse to work, hoping to force their employer to agree to their demands

subscription—an arrangement for providing continuing service, such as newspaper delivery, on a prepayment plan

suburban—referring to the outlying areas of a city or large town

vending—selling

DID YOU KNOW?

- The first newsboy, Bernard Flaherty, changed his name to Barney Williams and became one of the most famous American comedians of the 1800s.

- In 1992, the Walt Disney Company released the movie *Newsies*, a musical based on the 1899 newsboys' strike.

- At the 1904 World's Fair in St. Louis, a special day was held for newsboys; a Toledo businessman helped them start a national newsboys association.

- In January 1833, publisher Horace Greeley hired newsboys to deliver his new paper, the *New York Morning Post*. A huge blizzard made it hard to sell the paper, and Greeley stopped printing it a few weeks later.

- In 1852, Massachusetts became the first state to require all children to attend school. It took 66 years for other states to pass similar laws.

- Many newsboys wore distinct floppy caps with short brims. This style of hat is still worn by some people today.

43

IMPORTANT DATES

Timeline

1690	The first newspaper is published in America.
1833	Benjamin Day publishes the *New York Sun* and hires newsboys to sell the newspapers.
1854	The Children's Aid Society opens the Newsboys' Lodging House to shelter homeless boys; the first orphan trains leave New York City.
1899	New York City newsboys go on strike against two newspaper companies.
1938	The first national child-labor laws are passed but do not apply to newsboys.
1998	More adults than children and teens deliver newspapers to U.S. homes.

IMPORTANT PEOPLE

HORATIO ALGER (1832–1899)

Popular author of rags-to-riches stories that often featured newsboys as characters; wrote more than 130 novels but didn't become rich from his writing because he gave most of his money to homeless boys

CHARLES LORING BRACE (1826–1890)

Graduated from Yale in 1846 and from Union Theological Seminary in 1849; founded the Children's Aid Society, which provided help for newsboys and other orphans

HARRY E. BURROUGHS (1891– ?)

Former newsboy who became a lawyer and founded the Burroughs Newsboys Foundation in Boston

BENJAMIN HENRY DAY (1810–1889)

Lack of work led Day to begin publishing the Sun *in 1833; by 1835, the newspaper claimed a circulation of 19,360, the largest in the world*

JOHN CHRISTOPHER DRUMGOOLE (1816–1888)

Roman Catholic priest who ran the St. Vincent's Home for Homeless Newsboys in New York City

WANT TO KNOW MORE?

At the Library

Alger, Horatio. *Struggling Upward, or, Luke Larkin's Luck*. Mineola, N.Y.: Dover Publications, 1984.

Brown, Don. *Kid Blink Beats the World*. Brookfield, Conn.: Roaring Brook Press, 2004.

Oxlade, Chris. *Newspapers*. Chicago: Heinemann Library, 2002.

Pelusey, Michael, and Jane Pelusey. *Newspapers*. Philadelphia: Chelsea House, 2005.

On the Web

For more information on this topic, use FactHound.

1. Go to *www.facthound.com*

2. Type in this book ID: 075652458X

3. Click on the *Fetch It* button.

FactHound will find the best Web sites for you.

On the Road

The Children's Aid Society

105 E. 22nd St., Rm. 504
New York, NY 10010
212/949-4936
Founded by Charles Loring Brace in 1853; provides adoption and foster care to children and families of New York City

Newsboy Fountain Statue

Route 23 West, approximately ½ mile (0.8 km) from Route 7
Great Barrington, MA 01230
Statue of an anonymous newsboy with a newspaper in his hand, erected in 1895 and commissioned by William L. Brown, part owner of the first *New York Daily News*

Look for more We the People books about this era:

Angel Island
The Great Chicago Fire
Great Women of the Suffrage Movement
The Harlem Renaissance
The Haymarket Square Tragedy
The Hindenburg
Industrial America

The Johnstown Flood
The Lowell Mill Girls
The Orphan Trains
Roosevelt's Rough Riders
Women of the Harlem Renaissance
Yellow Journalism

A complete list of We the People titles is available on our Web site:
www.compasspointbooks.com

47

INDEX

About the Author

Michael Burgan is a freelance writer of books for children and adults. A history graduate of the University of Connecticut, he has written more than 100 fiction and nonfiction children's books. For adult audiences, he has written news articles, essays, and plays. Michael Burgan is a recipient of an Educational Press Association of America award.